Workplace Recipes: Coping with Unemployment and the Job You Hate

Joy Mouton

Table of Contents

Acknowledgement

This book is dedicated to the many family members and friends who have supported me over the years. I know I have prayed and received lots of prayers. I thank you and acknowledge you all for your love and support.
 I also dedicate this book to the new graduates and job seekers who struggle to search for their dream jobs. I initially realized my passion to help others when I became intrigued by my own career and inspired by professional interactions. I have had good job opportunities. I worked within many roles, ranging from entry-level to managerial. Over time, I met many people while working in various roles in retail, staffing, human resources, education, and consulting. Many people fantasize about something better, anything better. My goal and only hope is that the words in this book will inspire others to pursue their dreams, create new dreams, and become more understanding when confronted by others who are struggling to find theirs. I am familiar with the search, the value of self-awareness, a transition, and an open door. To you, I say keep going, keep trying. Tomorrow will be better.

First edition, 2008
ISBN 979-8-3507-1390-9 (ebook), ISBN 979-8-218-25517-6 (print)
Published by Career Wit, www.careerwit.com

Book Overview

All too infrequently is a book designed to express ways of coping from the perspective of one who has experienced job loss or company closing and transitioned. Years prior while working within a district managerial role, I was impacted by a layoff from a most admired company. Our only client filed bankruptcy. I accepted a severance package (what I affectionately call "a parting gift"). Part of the severance package included a life-altering meeting with a lackluster representative of an outplacement agency. On the meeting day, he entered the room and hurriedly announced he had another meeting to attend. Approximately five minutes later, I watched him exit. I left the meeting feeling worse than when I entered. This encounter needed to happen. It was one of many that opened my eyes and heart to become more compassionate towards others. Being present matters. Moving forward, I only accepted service-related jobs that allowed me to inspire and uplift in some way. I learned that many, like clients, "Carol" who felt despair after being released from a 20-year career or "John" who felt trapped in an uninspiring job and a lengthy job promotion process called a training cycle kept him learning more and advancing less. Accepting those jobs led me to creatively make a difference within a book.

This guide is an abbreviated toolkit for job seekers to limit frustration, cope and deal with feelings and issues linked to job separation and job dissatisfaction. This book is concurrently designed for parents and schools to coach young adults, new graduates, and job seekers who want to know how to survive in between jobs, locate suitable work, and for those workers who are amid miserable working conditions. Each chapter defines a different set of concepts uniquely tied into the goal to unify businesses and employees for the sake of a better workplace. Explore valuable resources and steps to allude to the recipe for success.

SECTION 1-The Job Seeker's Guide

Chapter One

Reaching Goals

Ever been to the local grocery market to buy 4 slices of bread, 3 batteries, 2 eggs, or a cup of milk? If you have, you quickly realized that you were forced to buy more or less; probably, not quite what you expected to bargain for on a budget. The "one size fits all" method works for some, but not for all. Fortunately for most of you, what you are about to read will satisfy your taste.

Leaving a job or separating from one can create feelings of worry, sadness, relief, and maybe anger. If you have these common feelings, they should only be temporary and not rule your everyday life. I felt compelled to share sources for time management and hope, to help you turn your experience into a positive encounter for a pathway to success. Part of the battle is discovering what to do next and what action to take in the meantime. You will find many of your answers in this single guide. Yet delightful, this brief guide is helpful to give you the tools you need to get started. First, let's begin by discussing basic principles that are sure to help you along the way to reaching your goals.

The effort taken with applying and setting goals is essential to the success of any individual, regardless of purpose. It is not likely that when you get in your car or on the bus, if you use public transportation, that you get in the seat without a destination, walking backwards and with your eyes closed. This may sound silly, but let's face it; there are not many people in our fast-paced communities who have the time, patience, or money, considering high gas prices, to drive aimlessly. If you find yourself riding aimlessly or wasting time during the day, it is most likely due to lack of planning, interest, and poor time management skills. Here you will find principles and tips to help you with your job search process or functioning on-the-job that you hate. There are four basic principles that can apply to everyday life.

Principle #1: Prepare

Set your standard and goals.

Everything begins with goals and preparation. During my journey, I wondered were there really differences between classes of people; if our outcome was directly related to our experience, and what others expect from us. Although we cannot always choose our family members, or our birth right, we can control and filter some situations; and make careful, non-hasty decisions. Abide by your rules. Whatever goals and rules you set, follow through. Recall the rules parents established in the household. They often aligned with goals and breaking them had consequences, perhaps, no video games, no parties, etc., effective and maybe painful. The lessons learned were "discipline"...to respect the rules, standards or face undesirable results. Likewise, when you set standards, you'll lay the foundation for a good relationship and preparation for at home or work. At your current or former place of business or if you were the owner of a company, notice there is an employee handbook. Its purpose is to set the proper expectations for a harmonious business relationship. The underlying message is that setting standards and goals embodies discipline and helps minimize chaos that is required for preparation.

Principle #2: Prioritize

Plan to win with timelines.

Establish your goals and commitment. This could mean to you gaining home ownership, a better job, or losing weight. Winning is based not only on setting goals, but utilizing resources and executing your plan. Avoid feeling overwhelmed by developing realistic timelines. For example, if you feel as though you are trapped in a cycle of unemployment blues or a dreaded job and find it ridiculously painful to arrive at work, take a route for job searching that requires planning an hour, day, or month at a time.

Daily Time Management Chart (Example)

Day XX
8:00 Attend breakfast/networking event (8-9am)
9:00
10:00 Send resumes to hiring companies
11:00 Call backs/follow-ups
12:00 Lunch (12-1pm)
1:00 Finish preparing for an interview
2:00
3:00 Interview (3-4:30pm)
4:00
5:00 Create thank you letter or card to send
6:00
7:00 Leisure/Hobby/Family time

If your circumstance is not so severe, your timelines can be lengthier; perhaps, monthly, annually, or 5-year plans may work for you. You will devote time to construct your plan. Most of us spend more time, even hours on social media than we do planning our futures.   What's wrong with that picture? Reaching your goals requires hard work. We cannot recall time or exchange it for a refund. Using apps, reminders and calendars can help. Your plan is simply just a plan, words spoken, thought, or written. Execute your plan. If you never plan, you will never do.

Principle #3: Be Positive

Watch your surroundings.

Locate or attract positive influences. Watch the company you keep. Not everyone wants to see you succeed and many may not approve of your decision, goal, or vision. Your mind is delicate and the foundation for your dream. In order to remain confident and focused, you will need to keep positive people in your corner and lose your so called, "friends" who may not have your best interest in heart. If you cannot lose them, then love them from a distance. Minimize the time you spend with them. If you do not have the support you need, look at others who are already in the position or role you want. Find your tribe.
Join or remain active in your civic, community, religious organizations or interest groups. You will find it beneficial for all. You do not always need others' blessings to become successful. You are designed to win. You can allow your success to be a surprise to you and them. Continue your walk. You have fate on your side.

Principle #4: Perseverance

Never give up.

You may not see instant success with the goal or set of goals you establish. After layoffs due to downsizing and company/plant closings, I reached most of my career and educational goals; not realizing that I would later find value in the journey. The journey itself allowed me to cultivate within the experience to share with others. Nothing happens by chance and long-term success takes vested time. Your reaction counts. Only you know how fulfilling life will be once you reach your goal or how unfulfilling it will be if you don't. Enjoy each day of your journey and be patient while you work towards victory. You are a work in progress just waiting and working toward your moment of success. It will happen.

Slogan for Success
Prepare, prioritize, and be positive to persevere for achievement.

Chapter Two

Coping in between Jobs, Entertainment, and ....$$Money

Waiting for your dream job can be a daunting experience. Idle time and idle minds are not good combinations. Always have an agenda. Each week should include a project that helps you get closer to reaching your goal. When you are busy, do not concentrate on what you do not have, what you cannot afford, or what you could be doing. Work with the tools and assignments at hand. Here are some tasks that may help you kill time and not your winning spirit.

Visit the Library
Taking a trip to the library and reading a book will take your mind off of your situation, temporarily. Sometimes, you will need an outlet. You do not want to turn into the cranky family member no one wants to meet after a long day. Books provide a sense of adventure, an escape while they offer knowledge. Haven't you heard? Books are no longer only found in paper back and hard cover versions. Yes, you can also read and listen online. You may learn something new and research a topic that appears interesting to you. The best thing about the library is that the visit is absolutely free. To locate a library in your area, visit www.usa.gov/libraries.

Explore the zoo, museum, park, or garden
The tourism guide and the city official websites usually have calendars of events that are child-friendly at no or little cost. Call for the times to verify accuracy of the information found online. Some museums and parks offer free performances, cultural events, theatrical plays, musicals, free displays of art certain times of the year, and other social events. The trip will help you unwind and

many of the events will be enjoyable for the entire family. If you start early enough, you can make it a day long tour and excursion.

Sharpen Your Skills

Take a course. There are a number of courses and seminars available. The YMCA and the Red Cross are a few options for taking life-saving courses, like CPR, swimming, or lifeguarding. Additional courses are offered at traditional colleges and universities; others on-demand and via remote, like at www.udemy.com, www.coursera.com and www.careerwit.com.
Knowledge can be everlasting and the skill you receive can help you land your next job or maybe save a life.

Volunteer

There is nothing like helping someone else in need to divert the attention off of you. Surely, each time you are asked by others, "Have you found a job, yet?" has made you nearly insane. Before you get to that stage, take time to help someone else in need. This may prove to be therapeutic for you. Likewise, the recipient will appreciate your effort and concern. There are so many devoted organizations, like United Way® and the Boys and Girls Club of America® that will allow you to help children, women, the aged, ill, and victims of natural disasters. Additionally, there are organizations that have ongoing recruiting and training for volunteers, like the Sodexho Foundation®, an organization that will train the unemployed to work for the non-profit to eliminate hunger in the nation. Do not limit yourself to national reach, your school or your children's school; your church may also need administrative or ministry assistance. Search for volunteer opportunities in your area at **1-800-VOLUNTEER.org.** Use your time to be productive.

Take Hobbies to Heart

Hobbies are a great way to spend your time and relax. Sometimes hobbies turn into careers. For example, ever heard of a baker or caterer who did not love to bake or entertain? When soul searching, some people decide on careers that they like solely based on skill. Try combining skill and hobby interest to explore your next career choice. Some hobbies may not be extremely lucrative; however, happiness is worth more than money. Do not underestimate the possibilities when jobless. Although career testing is available to help find a career match, you know what really matters to you and how you like to spend your time; in a dead-end job or in a job that you would commit to just because it is what you absolutely love to do.

Accept Temporary or Contract Assignments

You never thought you would have so much time. You have had spring cleaning sessions 5 times within the last month and you do not think you can endure another talk show, reality show, or daytime soap opera. It may be time to pursue contract opportunities. Venture into websites, like www.sologig.com, www.guru.com, www.flexjobs.com, www.ceweekly.com, www.wellfound.com, and staffing agencies, like Kelly Services®, www.kellyservices.com, one of the oldest and most reputable staffing firms.

Staffing firms help job seekers locate work with businesses that have job openings allowing job seekers to sample an industry or role prior to committing to it long term. This allows the businesses and the job seekers a chance to determine if the work relationships will be good fit for both. To select a local staffing agency, visit the official website for the American Staffing Association, www.americanstaffing.net, for inquiries. Some agencies will require registration prior to helping you. In some cases, be prepared to undergo testing to reveal your skill level for adequate placement. This placement process may not be an instant quick fix to resolving unemployment, but may be an option that can lead to career or industry transition, job recovery or a way to spend your valuable time.

Health and Fitness

The job search process typically involves submitting applications and resumes along with interviewing to compete for job openings. Maintain good health and healthy eating habits. You want to be physically and mentally prepared when you get a call for an interview. Consider fitness apps, like Blogilates and 7-Minute Workout. Consult with a doctor for the best results and check out the official website for the Federal Trade Commission (www.ftc.gov) for consumer protection information on dietary supplements, weight loss, and fraud.

Start a Business

An adventurer, Chris Guillebeau found a way to travel the world, and earn money concurrently documenting small business owners who started their businesses with only $100 at 100startup.com. One way to survive unemployment and employment gaps is to consider starting a business. When applying for jobs, expect to explain the gap of employment on applications and within interviews. As a human resources recruiter, I prescreened and interviewed a female candidate who indicated that she did "nothing" as she explained the gap of employment while blowing her bubbles with her bubble gum. Needless to say, that was not the best job catching, winning answer. Although I have provided ways to keep you occupied in between jobs, do not lose sight of the fact that you need to schedule and complete a job search. Account for your time. No hiring manager wants to hire an employee who is not resourceful or does not know how to properly manage time. You know the old cliché, "Money is time and time is money."

Write a Book & Share Skill

Release your passion. If you are skilled or talented and find yourself without a job; consider writing an article or book. Everybody has a story to tell. Both former President Barack and First Lady Michelle Obama have memoirs and books in print. Although impressive, you don't have to be the president or a celebrity to write. Writing and journaling is a healthy outlet. You just may have knowledge on a topic that others would find interesting and can prove to be profitable for you. You may become an acclaimed author addressing your favorite interests, your good or poor experiences, or write a how-to guide, thus creating a career for yourself writing or speaking. For example, Elizabeth Edwards, author and wife of a senator, wrote *Saving Graces,* a book that expresses desire to encourage and educate others with her first hand knowledge of fighting cancer. Another author and attorney, Cupcake Brown, turned her life story of overcoming unbelievable obstacles, including drug abuse, prostitution, homelessness into a book, *A Piece of Cake*. A negative experience can turn into a means for helping others and may allow extra money. Publishing a book can be made easy. There are many options to choose when publishing a book or sharing information, paperback, hardcover, audio, video, a workshop, and ebook publishing. Several resources can be located at www.ingramspark.com, www.thenovelry.com, www.livingwriter.com, www.copify.com, www.chapterly.com, www.authoritypublishing.com, and www.ibpa-online.org. These websites offer start-up information about writing, publishing, protecting, and marketing books and ebooks, including popular websites for listings to uncover the hidden market.

Over the years, you acquire many skills and some of them may be creative. Don't take for granted the skills that you can share by offering a class to others. Websites, like Skillshare®, Creative Live®, MasterClass®, and Teachable®, are a few of the many platforms that can help you promote or sell all types of courses.

Additionally, another way to use your voice is to consider doing freelance voice-overs, or narrating to earn extra money. Use your great voice to make audiobooks, commercials, cartoons, podcasts, courses, and video games. Find out more at Audible, VO Planet, Voices, Voice123, and Voice Crafters.

Revert back to the basics. Take advantage of opportunities to make money assisting others with daily tasks that may otherwise be taken for granted.

Here are a few ideas:
1. Cooking
2. Cleaning
3. Gardening
4. Pick-up/Delivery
5. Babysitting kids or caring for the elderly

For example, if you can do more than hold a fork in a kitchen, you may be able to profit from cooking and by writing a cookbook, cooking private dinners, catering for others or specializing in a special dish or dessert. Few people like to clean, but dirty work is necessary. Janitorial, lawn, transportation, sitting services will still be needed by people, individuals and families. You can start with your friends and family. They know your situation and will be willing to help.

One way that businesses generate growth, power, and wealth is through follow-ups and repeat business. Work your referrals. Do not be too proud to ask people you know for referrals. You may be surprised who is willing to help and the response you get just by asking. People buy from people they like, people they know, and sometimes buy from people who ask. Take a nostalgic marketing tip from your neighborhood girl scout.   Do you remember the visit to the grocery store or to your place of business? If so, you probably remember being approached by a Girl Scout to buy cookies; Or you were asked by a co-worker to purchase cookies for a fundraiser on behalf of a school, social, or charitable cause. Perhaps you were doing the selling or asking. Whatever the case, the sales grew nominally based on association and affiliation. Going back to the basics, lemonade and bake sales, reaching out and reaching back may be good for business.

For more information on business start-up, visit the Small Business Administration (www.sba.gov), for mentoring (www.score.org), and also search a comprehensive website for franchising, (www.franchoice.com). Learn about small business ownership from business owners by watching PBS' *Small Business School* or if you like more information 24-hours daily, the website choices for entrepreneurs are available to help you at www.smallbusinessschool.org www.forbes.com, and www.entrepreneur.com. Podcasts can also provide tips and expert business stories, like Honest HR, Mind Your Business, HBR IdeaCast, Work Life, How I Built This, TED Business, Problem Solvers, Masters of Scale, and Earn Your Leisure.

Managing your Money and Debt

Although, there is no perfect way to handle your finances and ration money between jobs, it is great to know that there is help out there. Utilize non-profit organizations within your community. They are willing to assist those experiencing hardship. Non-profit organizations lend helping hands and serve as wonderful resources for referrals to other agencies. Some organizations may assist with relief for utilities, housing, medical, school supplies, clothing, furniture, and even toys for children. Churches, food banks, family, and friends may allow you to join them for a meal as well. Avoid a lot of dining outside the home at cafes and restaurants. Light the fire on the barbecue pit, open can goods, create a spaghetti dish, or soup; meals that last longer than a single serving.

Create a Budget and Shopping List

Making do with few resources can be a challenge. Create a budget. Visit your bank's app, www.mvelopes.com or www.mint.intuit.com for free or low cost personal budgeting assistance. There are a number of tactics that you can use to make the transition easier. Before making purchases, map out a list of needed items and shop within your budget. Tackle priority items first. It will be useless to buy a new dress, try it on and wear it in the dark. Pay that utility bill first, ladies. He will understand if you do not have a new dress. Gentlemen, forget about the latest video game. Wash your own car. A little exercise will not hurt. Ladies love muscles. Avoid or postpone making impulse purchases and name brand items.

Using Coupons & Apps

Cutting and benefiting from coupons may have been a favorite past time for your mother, grandmother, or other relative, but many today continue to enjoy the value of coupons, loyalty, and rewards programs. I have an aunt who would not buy anything, unless it was on sale or she could save by using a coupon. Today, she is living well and continues saving with her coupons; something she says she will never abandon. I have saved. I have known her and others to save 70% or more on purchases due to the use of coupons and rewards programs. They are easy to use. Cut, scan, or print bar coded coupons from print ads and online websites or apps. Some coupons may not have a bar code; instead, they will have a string of letters or number/letter combination to enter to get the discount. Present coupons at the time of purchase. It's that easy!

Some stores will offer deals where free product promotions, like the "Buy one get one free" promotion can be likely. Everyone enjoys something free. There are many websites that provide free coupons, samples, and allow you to save money on groceries, visits to restaurants, and everyday products you use. You could be spending hundreds that you could otherwise save with the use of coupons or apps and get cash back.

To access and learn more about coupons or freebies, visit the following suggested websites:

www.coolsavings.com
www.infleuenster.com
www.coupons.com
www.valpak.com
www.couponcabin.com
www.fetch.com
www.gasbuddy.com
www.retailmenot.com
www.joinhoney.com

Coupons can be applied at the store front or online at established stores, like Target®, 1-800-Flowers.com®, WalMart®, and more. Some of the websites offer over 3,000 coupons, including discounts on health products, along with free samples, and gifts with purchases.
 Another option for eating and saving money is to use no waste food apps where restaurants or supermarkets send extra or near expired food to social service agencies to be dispersed to the public. This is a great way to get food from some of the best restaurants and grocery stores free or deeply discounted. Check out apps like, Food Rescue, Flashfood, Too Good to Go, City Harvest, and Misfits Market. Let's not forget about some of your fast food or fast casual dining

restaurants that offer rewards. Dunkin®, Chili's®, Mod Pizza®, and Chick-fil-A® are among some of the participating businesses with active app-based rewards programs.

Savings

Pay yourself first. Utilize money in your savings account or retirement account, like 401K wisely, if at all. If you do not have a savings account, take a shopping trip around your living quarters, house or apartment, garage, or storage area. Survey your belongings. Gather all duplicated items; items you have no use for today, and items you have never used. Stop hanging onto that size 3 skirt or old sweater that you retired 15-20 years ago. That's called "vintage" now, a treasure. Organize a garage sale. You do not have to own a garage to do so. Online marketplaces, like Poshmark®, Mercari®, or eBay®, which is one of the largest global marketplace, "garage sale" is excellent to sell gently used and new products or your "junk". Find your camera and photograph your items for placement and view and sale online. Become a merchant at an established online marketplace or establish your own website. If you decide to develop your own website, options, like Wix® and Spotify® offer some of the best web-based tools. Most software companies offer information about payment or transaction processing, and shopping cart programs. However, if you need to identify more information about accepting payments or payment process management companies, visit www.paypal.com, www.squareup.com, www.verisign.com, and www.cybersource.com to begin your search. Before you place your product online for sale, do not forget everything you know and have learned about safety and marketing. The price is just as important as the place, the location and products you choose to sell. Make sure you price each item considering the small fee that the payment transaction management company assesses for online transactions. If you can sell items, you can sell yourself for your next job opportunity. Tie this task into your personal marketing plan or career search strategy, especially if you are seeking a job in sales and marketing. In addition to managing time and your job search, manage your money. Do not forget to open an emergency savings account and store the money to use should times get really hard.

Financial Literacy

Seek advice from a financial expert or agency. Check a directory or planner, like investors.gov if you want to try investing only if you have excess. Look for a credit counselor and bankruptcy attorney, if your situation is really serious. After all, this is your future we are talking about here.

Counselors will be able to help reduce payments to your debtors, negotiate payment, and help prevent outstanding debt from reoccurring. This type of service is usually free or offered at a reduced cost with agencies, like Consumer Credit Counseling Services and Credit Solutions. Debt settlement and debt consolidation companies usually offer a free consultation and interactive calculator to help with debt reduction and debt management over a period of time. Learn more about financial literacy or gain detail at www.mymoney.gov, www.cccsintl.org or www.creditsolutions.com.

When discussing your financial matters with an attorney, determine if liquidating all assets or if salvaging a portion of your assets will be necessary. This is referred to as filing bankruptcy, Chapter 7 or Chapter 13. Filing bankruptcy should not be taken lightly. It should be given serious thought. Know the consequences of the decision you make.

Another way to improve your financial situation, if you are a homeowner, consult with a lender about your options, pros and cons for refinancing your home. Lastly, listen to podcasts, access guides, or take a free financial course (www.fdic.gov). Use this time for new beginnings. Do not fret over the past. Move forward knowing that you have work to do and dreams to be made. Remain driven.

Section 2: Surviving the "Jungle" at Work

Chapter Three

Business Etiquette

Perception is reality. When a company defines its culture and expectations, hiring managers and recruiters seek the candidate who is most qualified based on skill set and cultural fit. Your image, perception, and popular opinion mean a lot. A second chance may not be guaranteed. Your ex-boyfriend or girlfriend may be given a second chance, but when searching for a job, that mandate may not apply.

Take a few moments to think about your past relationships, place of business, former employers, and ask yourself, "Why you decided to separate?" Our needs change, our employers' process or business needs change and perception of others change or are influenced. Sometimes there are things that we cannot control. However, image is not one of them. Like dating, interviewing has become so intricate; we have seen interviewing and recruiting conducted online and on television with competitions, like American Idol, The Voice, and on The Apprentice. Even a former business president, Donald Trump's famed show was centered on the idea of a very public and lengthy group interview, sometimes referred to as a behavioral style "panel interview". For those who are unfamiliar, the show featured a series of assignments, usually team-oriented that required coordination, time management, and mental competency to endure. The winner took all, the "dream job," publicity and all the many perks that come along with working within an executive- level role. Through this show, viewers could see how marketing campaigns are implemented and what companies really want in job applicants. Not bad for a one-hour reality show. At first glance, it was noticeable that all of the contestants (interviewers) were professionals, business savvy, with polished demeanor, great communication skills, and team-oriented; all skills that employers admire and desire from their employees. You too can have a professional image and without beating your budget to death. Understand that searching for a job is a job and can get costly in the process.

When you are job hunting, your physical appearance is linked to your image and how people perceive you. The standard dress code for interviewing is a tailored suit, often professional clothing. If you are trying to feed a family or just survive with the basic necessities with limited funds to purchase anything new; less is always more. You want to always get the most for your money, without skipping quality.

 Locate the clothing you need to make a positive impression. Consider your search for "free" or "sale" items at:
1. Thrift and resale shops
2. Discount stores and some department stores
3. Local non-profit agencies
4. Churches
5. Friends and family

A number of organizations offer gently used clothing, like ThredUp, Goodwill Industries® and Dress for Success® to name a few. Check your local discount stores, which are stores that inherit past season merchandise from well-known department stores and sell them at lower prices. Depending on the time of the year, department store clearance racks may have great deals on clothing, shoes, and accessories, like jewelry, ties, and more. KOHL's® and Macy's® are a few department stores during sale time that may offer great bargains.

Some examples of discount stores include Ross®, Marshall's®, Burlington's®, and T.J.Maxx®. Good quality clothing for the workplace is often priced under $40. Look for stores that are going out of business, outlets, and clearance centers. Reasonably priced unused clothing may prove beneficial anytime, especially during penny pinching times.

Colors and Culture at Work

Beware of your color choices. Colors are beautiful in a garden or a rainbow, not always the best choice for a formal business meeting or interview. Colors can affect memory, performance, and purchases. Before you make your choice for wardrobe at work for an interview or business meeting, study the workplace culture. If the company is considered on the cutting edge, innovative in nature, a less conservative appeal may be acceptable. On the other hand, if you are unsure of the recruiter's or hiring manager's perception, stick with the traditional basics, black, navy blue, or gray or some conservative color for virtual meetings. Here is an idea of the *Meaning of Color* in our American culture.

RED= Associated with passion, love, warning, and energy

BLACK= Symbolizes sophistication, seriousness, power, elegance

ORANGE= Excitement, stimulating, cheerful

GREEN=Promotes growth, prosperity

BLUE= Related to serenity, trust, wisdom

PURPLE= Majestic, royalty, mysterious

WHITE= Clean, pure, good
*See The Meaning of Color, www.colormatters.com and www.color-wheel-pro.com for additional information.

The next time you select clothing, consider what colors say about you. You may announce your personality subliminally through color. Implications can be detrimental to how others view you and may affect your achievement.

Additionally, with the widespread international influence and jobs going global, knowledge of the effects of culture in theory will need to be included in your preparation for a job here and abroad. I can sum it up in one term, "diversity."

Employers will need its employees to understand that American and popular culture will not be identical to culture and values that exist in other countries. Gender differences are recognized in other cultures and countries. For instance, women may be required to wear clothing and colors that adorn the *entire* body in other countries. Concurrently, women may also be less visible in male dominating roles and more submissively viewed. Fashion may follow that perspective.

In the United States, there are differences recognized in fashion at work. Notice that typically, employee handbooks and guides contain explicit definitions of how to conduct orderly and professionally at work. Some companies may not have a stated dress code policy.

However, consider a more traditional professional approach during meetings and interviews, similar to the following:

Clothing	Acceptable	Not Acceptable
Women		
Collared shirts	X	
Blouses/Sweaters	X	
Knee length skirts	X	
Sleeveless shirts		X
Chiffon/Shear wear		X
Leggings/Stirrup pants (spandex wear)		X
Men		
Pants	X	
Collared Shirts/Sweaters	X	
Ties	X	
Blazers/Suits	X	
Misc.		
Suits/Blazers	X	
Workout/Athletic Gear/Sneakers		X
Shorts		X
Sandals (Open toe)		X
Beach wear (halter/low cuts/		X

Some standard dress codes may be more casually flexible, gender neutral, allowing you to apply your personality through fashion, and permitting seasonal dress codes for employees in the alignment with corporate structure.

The dress code and colors seen at work are important to address the company's expectations. Of course, this is all relevant to us as we are found employed with companies that are catering to the evolving talent pool and target customer in America. However, I have yet to see a dress code policy that mirrors the trendy images found on BET, VH1, or MTV. If your style replicates images likely to be found on a music video or barely dressed artists. Leave that trend at home on workdays and during interviews. Cover it up, babe. Resort to professionalism in your demeanor and attire at work.

So, you have been consistent with searching for a job. You have interviewed, negotiated your compensation and acquired the ultimate job. Way to go! Now, you find there is new management and the smile you wore, like a child on a birthday or Christmas morning has faded. You ask yourself again, "What's next?"

Creating Harmony at Work

Chapter Four

Finding Peace

Companies can choose to downsize, reorganize, close, or make a number of operational changes resulting in uneasiness in the office. Find peace even with tradeoffs. There are common reasons employees choose to locate another job opportunity. Some of them include: better pay, poor management, burnout, more convenient location, and better work hours or conditions. If you share any of these feelings, visit www.pbs.org/livelihood to discover that you are not alone. PBS offers a platform for releasing frustrations. *Livelihood* covers topics that affect workers through video, online, and some versions aired on PBS; all are helpful to educate on trends and tips for solutions at work. Likewise, people all over the world vent on social media platforms, Twitter and Instagram, mostly not anonymously after a break-up, disappointments, a long dragging day at work, or for any little irritant that the day may bring. Tuning in or voicing your opinion may help to cure the stress that your co-workers, customers or boss caused earlier during the day and may prolong your decision to locate work elsewhere. Griping publicly may not be a good idea. Be careful with your comments before broadcasting to the world; after all, it is called the "*world wide web*". A different option to get workplace answers or find some commonality or comfort may be to listen to podcasts, like Your Next Move, ZigZag, and The Good Life Project. Certain podcasts address problems at work, share a few good stories; some for entertainment and for guidance. Only accept advice from experts. In the end, no podcast can convince you to stay married to your job. Only you know what is working for you.

Before you make your decision to jump ship to look for another job, ask lots of questions to the HR professional, employees or former employees. Research the company's culture. In addition to researching reputable career and business magazines, some choose to research blogs, reviews, and websites like, Indeed, Glass Door, LinkedIn for some insight or to find jobs. If you take that route, be discerning about the content.

Some of you are not unemployed, but actively looking for a different, better opportunity. While waiting for your "dream job," make the best of your situation. Although no career is perfect, you definitely do not want to resign and later have remorse because you located another boss or employer much worse than the previous one; Or find yourself working for the boss, like the one who went old school at the ice treats shop, pleaded guilty for spanking employees for doing an "unsatisfactory" job at work or just as bad, if not worse, you could work for the pervert retailer boss who strips down regularly at work and parades around the office in his under garments as a practice of "standard operating procedure." Making the decision to begin a job search requires thought. Be confident and secretive with your decision.

There are steps that you can take before making the big decision and signs that will help you make the best decision for your situation. Some of the strategies outlined I used and made suggestions to others over the years to help with coping with the job before the dream job. I refer to the steps as the "10 Steps to Surviving the Workplace Jungle."

10 Steps to Surviving the Workplace Jungle

1. *Think what life would be like without a job.*

You have probably endured a much worse situation in the past. During my lowest points, I have reached back into my past experiences to help me go beyond my struggle to overcome a dilemma. I also would think about a friend, "Carl," who has spent over 30 years of his life carrying a life-threatening illness. I recall a particular conversation he and I had when he said that all he wanted was to be healthy. This was a fair request, considering he could not remember a time in his adult life that was absent from hospitalization or a doctor's visit. He just wants a "normal life," a steady job, a family one day; life experiences that are taken for granted by most. Whatever your hardship, think of a familiar situation that will be uplifting to you; Or think about a friend or relative's situation, the one worse than yours. If you do not have one, think about "Carl" or turn on the news. I am sure you will be able to find one there. Be grateful for where you are now. Consider the fact that your condition is only temporary. You are just visiting and so is your condition.

2. *Develop better professional relationships.*

Join a mentorship program or help to create a program at your company. If you work with irate customers and difficult co-workers, change the way you refer to them. Think of them as your friends who have problems and they have chosen you to help. You then become the problem solver, an advisor with their best interest in mind. Determine underlying reasons for discontent. Be slow to anger. Avoid becoming defensive and

help them confidentially resolve their problems.   Always
follow up. That's what friends do.

3. Make reference to the reason you accepted the job.

Do you remember the excitement you had when the manager
or hiring personnel extended the job offer to you? Professional
marketers rely on your feelings, senses, and desires to sell you
products that you may not need.
They make the products so appealing that you cannot resist
and when sales representatives observe your hesitation, they
make reference to the benefits or characteristics that made the
products appealing to you to convince you to purchase by
concentrating on your interest. For example, food restaurants,
like McDonald's® tend to advertise near meal time to stimulate
hunger and feed on your physiological or emotional need and
solve that need. They show menu items, like fries, burgers,
and salad on television. The colors are so vibrant you can
almost smell the food cooking and taste it. You then become a
hungry customer.
At your place of business, you may have good days and not so
good days. Expect that; but how you manage those days and
react will make all the difference. Focus on why you accepted
the job and why you are there (to pay your bills, fulfill
customers' needs, support your family), and you will find
purpose in what you do. Little annoyances and irritants won't
matter. It's not all about you.

4. Make work fun and interesting.

 The company's culture is defined by the founder and implemented by human resource professionals, managers, and you, the employee. Your duty is to be compliant. Make work interesting enough to be an outstanding performer. Prioritize by completing the tedious task you dislike most first or the tasks that have close deadlines. If you lack challenging assignments, request more stimulating work from your manager. Volunteer to help a co-worker. Helping a co-worker is also an awesome way to build a better professional relationship. Everybody likes the team player. You spend more time at work than with your family. It would be nice to get along with your "extended family members." If your company allows it, bring a small radio and keep the volume low, just above a whisper to eliminate distractions. Participate in contests and competitions. Sometimes contests and reward programs help employees remain motivated to drive performance results.

5. Improve your communication skills.

Avoid chaos and definitely *do not* create it. Revert back to the days your parents may have told you to not say anything if you do not have anything nice to say. Volunteer to conduct a team meeting. Think and rehearse your words before you say or write them. Watch your tone at all times. Apologies do not really erase the underlying message. If you think before you speak, you will avoid offending your co-workers. The last thing you want to do is offend the one employee who later becomes your boss. If you need extra help, check with colleges and universities or local newspapers for seminars and continuing education courses to help you improve.

6. Keep the faith.

Store your favorite inspirational song or quote nearby. Recite it before starting each day. Challenge yourself to complete atleast one unselfish act or go beyond the call of duty on any given day. Meditate and pray. I always remember my grandmother saying, "Prayer is powerful." When we undergo trying times, power in prayer takes on a new meaning. Unfortunately, a value that is seemingly more relative during a struggle than any other time.

7. Take advantage of company benefits and perks.

Become familiar with your benefits. Some companies offer fitness plans and discounts, onsite fitness facilities, event tickets, and more. If you find yourself suffering from burnout, visit the doctor for a physical or ask about flexible scheduling. Utilize your vacation time. It is better to give 100% effort than poor service and partial effort any time. Your thoughts and feelings inside reflect what others see outside. Customers can see smiles and hear frustration.

8. Volunteer and attend company functions.

Represent your company as a member of a committee or interest group, like inclusion and diversity programs. Attend fundraisers for non-profit organizations, like the March of Dimes walk-a-thons or marathons. Attend and encourage team outings, workshop attendance, or suggest potluck dinner parties for your department.

9. Relieve your stress.

Breathe, exhale, and relax. Indulge in a healthy diet. Eat breakfast. Include fresh fruit, vegetables, protein and vitamins in your regimen. Exercise is also a great stress reliever. Gain a gym membership for working out. Locate a few co-workers or friends willing to take a brisk walk. Hire a personal fitness trainer. Take a dance, yoga, or aerobics class. Hit the court for a game of basketball or tennis. Visit online for special programs and consult with your doctor before starting any diet or exercise program.

10. Break the routine.

If you get tired of the routine, find a new one. Complete assignments in a different order. Find a new route to work. Have lunch with a friend, spouse, or family member. Add a hobby. Work on a personal goal. Balance your work/family life. Do not accept more responsibility than you can handle. Share responsibility. Attend a networking event. Take a dance class. Make some new friends.

 If you try these suggestions and do not find job satisfaction, it may be time to locate a new job. Let's explore further. Outlined are the 8 Signs that indicate it is time to find another job.

8 Signs to Determine its Time to Find Another Job

1. You walk to work because you can't afford to buy gas or anything else.

2. You have a wandering mind, thinking about what's next on Oprah (OWN), thinking about a vacation during a department meeting, or while your boss is speaking.

3. You suddenly get ill or feel sick before its time to report to work.

4. You are the only one left because your boss and your co-workers have all quit before you.

5. The job you want doesn't exist or someone has it and must retire in 50 years for you to get it.

6. You do not have time to think about anything else.

7. Nothing makes sense $$ anymore.

8. You forget your way to work.

If you can relate to one or more of the 8 signs, it is time to plan your escape. Return immediately to the beginning of this book, reread. Apply the suggestions until you locate your dream job with the help of a career services firm, or training organization, like Career Wit (www.careerwit.com). Typically, these firms help with career management support, like leadership or professional development, resume writing, interview preparation, upskilling, and business etiquette which will get you on a fast track to your career path to help you reach your life altering goals. Keep the faith. Do not allow pride to block your path to success.

The moral of this guide has been to share needed tools and motivation to help you thrive during moments of unbearable unemployment status or to assist you with sustaining at work when your existence there has become too difficult for comfort. The truth is that we can have many layers, interests, and talents that co-exist. Self-discovery does not have to be painful, but an adventurous journey as life unfolds. Life can include unexpected experiences, interruptions and twists of outcomes. The problem is that often we imagine the career route like the theme and anticipated ending of a novel. Disappointment occurs when results do not happen quickly or in the way imagined. Unexpected outcomes can still be promising. I would have never imagined writing or public speaking as skills heavily used within my career. I was the shy student who most never heard my voice because I was too shy to talk or respond to questions during class meetings. Yet, taking inventory of skills, knowledge and interests can pave opportunity. A career is a set of jobs. If you are in motion, you are on track. Your dream job could be provided or the one you create.

Break the cycle of selecting the wrong employer or the "it will do" career. There are many pathways that can drive results. The first step is deciding to make a change in you.

Change is expected to be embraced at work and at home; but one thing that will never change in life is our *ability* to change to reach our goals through the application and the adoption of a positive attitude, planning, the will to try, and the relentless desire to accomplish greatness.

Slogan for Success:
Prepare, prioritize, and be positive to persevere for achievement.
Joy Mouton- American Author

Directory of Resources for Job Seekers

With so many options, job searching can be overwhelming. Time is of the essence; thus, selecting the right mix to create your job search strategy is optimal to landing your desired job. This section is an abbreviated single directory of resources that will aid with your job search and assist with organizations that offer resources for your special circumstances. Most websites and organizations have national representation that support the homeless, temporarily unemployed, veterans, children, the elderly, and physically challenged (persons with disabilities). Check with the following job boards, your local governmental agencies, libraries, fraternal organizations, and local chapter or national professional associations for more information.

Federal Agencies

These agencies offer varied programs for food, housing, health, employment, transitional, and temporary assistance.

State Offices of Veteran's Affairs	*www.va.gov*
Department of Labor	*www.dol.gov*
Social Security Administration	*www.ssa.gov*
Department of Housing and Urban Development	*www.hud.gov*
Department of Health and Human Services	*www.hhs.gov*
Department of Justice (Civil Rights/Disabilities)	*www.ada.gov*

Charitable Service Organizations
www.charitynavigator.org
Directory of non-profit organizations, includes top ten lists. Select by category (ex: Education, Human Services, Religion, Health, Arts, International, etc.)
www.nationalhomeless.org/local
A network of service providers to aid the homeless in the United States.

Medical
www.pparx.org
Partnership for Prescription Assistance gives assistance for medical prescription needs.

www.ask.hrsa.gov/pc/
Medical and clinic locator offers good sources for those without health insurance coverage and limited money for healthcare expenses.

Legal
http://www.abanet.org/legalservices/probono/directory/programlinks.html
American Bar Association may offer sources for reduced cost legal aid.

www.prepaidlegal.com
Affordable, members' only legal insurance for legal assistance.

Housing
Whether paying a mortgage or renting, if there is a challenge with paying or the possibility of eviction or jo money for repairs, know which agencies might be able to help. Some of them listed are charitable agencies, like Habitat for Humanity and others.
www.habitat.org
Habitat for Humanity is a religious non-profit organization that pulls together all, regardless of religious preference, for the purpose of eliminating homelessness through delivering affordable, low cost housing.

More Helpful Resources
www.apartments.com
www.nlihc.org
www.hud.gov

Food
Check with local authorities, churches, and associations. There are many food pantries available for disaster relief and year round assistance.
www.secondharvest.org
National network of over 200 food banks and food rescue organizations.

www.mowaa.org
Meals on Wheels Association of America (MOWAA) offers nutritional services to Americans, including meals and grants to seniors across the country.

Public Transportation & Auto Service
Accessing transportation and auto repairs could become problematic when on a budget. There are a number or programs for low income, seniors, the sick, and people with disabilities to help with transportation to doctor's appointments and for other needs. Call 211. www.publictransportation.org.
www.wrenchitforwardlbk.org
www.findhelp.org
www.autocarehaven.org
www.theliftgarage.org
www.fixitforard.org

Communication Resources (Free voicemail and Email accounts or other mailbox options)
www.gmail.com
www.outlook.com
www.icloud.com
www.usps.gov

Computer Resources (Computer Use, Repair, Free downloads)
www.usa.gov/libraries
www.geeksquad.com
www.pcworld.com
www.sharetechnology.com

Counseling (Directories of churches, licensed professionals, and therapists)
www.worshipquest.org
www.counseling.org
www.psychologytoday.com
www.therapeuticdirectory.com

Money Management and Financial Literacy
www.mymoney.gov
A website that offers information from the American Institute of Certified Public Accountants and issues free toolkits on money management and financial education. Topics include; budgeting, saving and investing, credit management, and paying for education. Order free tool kits at 1-888-696-6639.

Clothing and Grooming
www.beautyschoolsdirectory.com
Directory of schools in the United States and Canada that offer services ranging from cosmetology, barbering, nails, and skin care and makeup. These schools may offer discounts or specials for

grooming offered by students. This is a great option for grooming while on a budget.

www.dressforsuccess.com
Dress for Success is an organization that supplies gently used and new clothing for those in need, perfect for interviewing to locate suitable employment.

Career Management & Training
www.careerwit.com
Texas based career management and training consulting firm dedicated to servicing job seekers, and businesses in search of them with consultant-led and self-study training programs, workshops, books, and virtual self-service centers.

Resume Creation, Distribution, and References
www.resumeblaster.com
www.resumerabbit.com
www.myperfectresume.com
www.recruiter.com
www.resumetarget.com
www.references-etc.com

General Boards and Job Announcements
www.careerbuilder.com
www.monster.com
www.truecareers.com
www.simplyhired.com
www.collegegrad.com
www.jobboom.com
www.careercity.com
www.indeed.com

More Job Boards

www.coolworks.com
www.ziprecruiter.com
www.glassdoor.com
www.getwork.com
www.flexjobs.com
www.linkedin.com

Diversity Job Boards

www.hirediversity.com
www.fortyplus.org
www.jobs40plus.com
www.seniors4hire.org
www.wiseworker.com

Technical and Telecommunications Job Boards

www.telecomcareers.com
www.mobilejobtalk.com
www.computerjobs.com
www.computerwork.com
www.pathwystotechnology.com
www.itpinnacle.com
www.dice.com
www.techcareers.com
www.techfetch.com

Pharmaceuticals/Science/ Engineering Job Boards

www.pharmadiversityjobboard.com
www.engcen.com
www.engineerjobs.com

More Job Boards
www.industrialengineer.com
www.mechanicalengineer.com
www.physlink.com/jobs
www.aquaticnetwork.com
www.biospace.com
www.medzilla.com
www.pharmaopportunities.com

Staffing and Human Resources Job Boards
www.staffingjobs.com
www.jobs4hr.com
www.stafflink.net
www.hrcrossing.com
www.ihirehr.com

Arts and Entertainment Job Boards
www.voiceofdance.com
www.musicalonline.com
www.voiceofdance.com
www.musicalonline.com
www.entertainmentcareers.net
www.artjob.org

Consulting Job Boards
www.econsultants.com
www.upwork.com
www.freelancer.com
www.cyberstaff.com
www.gofreelance.com
www.globaleducationandmanagementconsulting.com

International & Cruise Job Boards
www.jobserve.com
www.allcruisejobs.com
www.carribbeanjobs.com

Manufacturing and Mining Job Boards
www.jobsinmanufacturing.com
www.manufacturingjobs.com
www.steelonthenet.com
www.forestryusa.com

Construction Job Boards
www.constructionjobsource.com
www.constructionjobs.com
www.constructionwork.com
www.ihireconstruction.com
www.craftstaffing.com
www.constructionjobstore.com

Finance Job Boards
www.jobsinthemoney.com
www.efinancecareers.com
www.creditjobstoday.com
www.creditjobs.com

Energy Job Boards
www.greenjobs.com
www.energyjobs.com
www.professionalenergyjobs.com

Government and Military Job Boards
www.911jobs.com
www.hrsfederaljob.com
www.militaryexits.com

More Job Boards
www.usmilitary.com
www.militaryjobzone.com
www.militarycareers.com

Transportation and Distribution Job Boards
www.flightglobal.com/jobs
www.airjobsdaily.com
www.jobsinlogistics.com
www.transittalent.com
www.railjobs.com
www.lyft.com
www.railroadjobs.com
www.instacart.com

Travel and Leisure Job Boards
www.meetingjobs.com
www.resortjobs.com
www.spajobs.com

Retail and Fashion Job Boards
www.fashioncareercenter.com
www.allretailjobs.com
www.workinretail.com
www.stitchfix.com
www.hsn.com
www.peopleready.com
www.retailstaffingsolutions.com

Sales and Marketing Job Boards
www.salesjobs.com
www.prcrossing.com
www.marketingcrossing.com
www.massreps.com

More Job Boards
www.acareerinsales.com
www.salesanimals.com
www.marketingjobs.com

Automotive Job Boards
www.automotivejobs.com
www.needtechs.com
www.autojobbank.com
www.bestautojobs.com

Sports and Entertainment Job Boards
www.entertainmentcareers.net
www.sportsjobsusa.com
www.collegesportscareers.com
www.tennisjobs.com
www.jobsinsports.com
www.workinsports.com
www.sportsjobsusa.com
www.collegesportscareers.com
www.tennisjobs.com

Writing and Publishing Job Boards
www.bookjobs.com
www.constant-content.com
www.writejobs.com
www.mediabistro.com
www.problogger.com
www.journalismjobs.com
www.bloggingpro.com
www.freelancewriting.com
www.copify.com
www.smartblogger.com

Real Estate Job Boards
www.realestatejobs.com
www.nar.com
www.real-jobs.com

Insurance Job Boards
www.greatinsurancejobs.com
www.insurancejobs.com
www.insuranceworkforce.com
www.ultimateinsurancejobs.com

Education (GED, Colleges and Universities)

In order to reach your career goals, you may find that your level of education or lack of an education may affect your chances for achieving your desired career goal. Education provides more choices for those who choose to commit to studying. A student guide can be obtained free of charge from the U.S. Department of Education 1-800-433-3243 or www.ed.gov/prog .

National Association for College Admissions Counseling
www.nacanet.org
National Association for College Admissions Counseling offers a free booklet and information on student resources, online resources, professional development, and scholarship scams. National college fairs are coordinated and scheduled nationwide to aid with the college selection process. Visit the official website for detail.

www.acenet.edu
GED Testing-American Council on Education contains information regarding adult learner programs and testing service initiatives listed by state.

Colleges and Universities
Directories of colleges and universities can be located by visiting the following websites:

www.worldwidelearn.com

www.classesusa.com/schools

www.college.us.com

Online Education
Technology has changed the setting for learning without compromising the quality of education. Online, correspondence course attendance has become one of the most convenient methods of completing a course or degree. This convenience gives universities, like the University of Phoenix, the largest private institution, leverage in enrollment and excellence in education while meeting students' needs. Visit the following websites to research and find a course or degree plan that will be beneficial for the pursuit of your or your child's career.

www.educationcentral.com

www.college.com

www.coursera.com

Financing College
The following websites offer educational resources, particularly, for calculating costs of admissions and financing your educational goals after you have broken the piggy bank or before you do.

www.fafsa.gov

www.collegedata.com

www.fastweb.com

www.scholarshipowl.com

www.collegeispossible.org

www.collegeboard.org

www.scholarships.com

www.militaryscholar.org

www.bold.org

www.myscholly.com

Other Helpful Websites

www.rams.com/srn/execsrch.htm

www.college.net

www.acenet.edu/programs/HEATH

www.uscg.mil

www.military.com

Loan Forgiveness (Programs available to assist with lessening the burden of loan repayment)

www.ed.gov

www.finaid.org

5 Best Careers for Stability

These career picks were selected based on some of our basic human needs. We should all want and need food, good healthcare, and thirst for knowledge to gain a better quality of life and achievement.

1- Teacher
2- Nurse
3- Mental Health Counselor
4- Chef/Food Manager
5- Technical Engineer

The first pick, education is one of the few fields that maintains during all turmoil and trends. Its long-standing ability makes it among the top of the list for career picks for sure career stability. Careers in education can range from instructors, principals, counselors, coaches, administrators, and more. Nevertheless, teachers help to control every child's road. Our teachers cultivate, motivate and drive the leaders of every generation with no avail and minimal compensation for the value of the work they do. I have many favorite teachers from all grade levels, including high school, college, and graduate school. However, like me, many of you may be able to find some of the best teachers at home or within your communities. I watched many of my family members and my best friend give much of their time unselfishly, and admirably working weekends and long days, spending their own money, feeding energy and support to students who may not have otherwise received the love and wisdom they needed to graduate and become productive citizens. Many of their students are old enough to have followed in their footsteps and have by becoming educators; the manifestation of the "each one, teach one" model.

Job #1

Teacher

Educational Requirements (minimum): Undergraduate degree, certification or state licensing (Emergency Certification and Alternative programs may be available)

Salary Range: $43-61K Varies by # of years of experience, grade level teaching, setting or district (www.dol.gov)

Job Overview:

Motivate, lead, assess, and direct child and adult learners on a single subject or many subjects to help with development of critical thinking, life, and social skills. Teachers help provide the foundation and preparation for adjustment into the real world for the future. Must be able to work with diverse groups and address student needs, physical and mental. Typically, teachers work 10-month year, with a 2-month break. Some teachers work part time or additional jobs to supplement their income and use summers for continuing education. Licensing requires continued studies and workshop participation, for more information, current trends and updates to impact students.

Helpful Websites

Recruiting Teachers, Inc.
www.recruitingteachers.org

National Council for Accreditation of Teacher Education
www.ncate.org

National Center for Alternative Certification
www.teach-now.org

More Helpful Websites
Association for Career and Technical Education
www.acteonline.org

National Association for the Education of Young Children
www.naeyc.org

Council for Professional Recognition
www.cdacouncil.org

American Federation of Teachers
www.aft.org

National Education Association
www.nea.org

Education America
www.educationamerica.net

Teach Abroad
www.teachermania.com

Jobs in Education
www.teachersatwork.com

www.education-jobs.com

www.teachers.net

www.teachingjobs.com

www.teachersonline.com

More Jobs in Education

www.recruitingteachers.org

www.usteach.com

www.teachermania.com

www.studentaffairs.com

www.collegejobs.com

www.academic360.com

www.academickeys.com

www.teachers-teachers.com

www.jobsinschools.com

www.myeducationcareer.com

www.eslemployment.com

www.eslworldwide.com

Job Opportunities at Colleges and Universities

www.chronicle.com

www.trainerquest.com

www.higheredjobs.com

More Job Opportunities
www.adjunctadvocate.com

www.toseeka.com

www.phd.org

Directory of Schools
Colleges, Universities, Private and Public-School Locator
National Center for Education Statistics
www.nces.ed.gov/globallocator

Job #2

Nurse

The next career selected among the best for job stability is nursing. Nursing has come a long way since the days of the mid-wife, private home nursing before the times of hospitalization. Do not be surprised if you find yourself sitting next to one on an airplane. There are traveling nurses who rotate from city to city or from hospital to clinic to assist with the care of patients. Just as Barbie® has transformed and upgraded to reflect today's fashion; gone are the sparkling white uniforms that nurses once wore. Their fashion forward uniforms can be located in rainbow colors found online and in a store front for purchasing. Not only are nurses working with big hearts, but looking good while committing to their profession. A career in nursing and healthcare can be rewarding in many ways, but the most rewarding is the fact that they partake in a role to save lives every day, despite, not quite having the luxury of what many in other careers have, a "typical day." If you are looking to work a boring job, without challenge, where every minute is predicted, a career in nursing or working in healthcare may not be for you. This career is for serious inquiries only.

Educational Requirements (minimum): Degree and licensing
Salary Range: $49,000 -113,930K or substantial based on occupation and setting
(www.dol.gov)
Job Overview:

Healthcare and Allied Health hold opportunities for many who have genuine concern to research for cures, prevent illness and disease, and aid the ill. Typical careers include physicians, surgeons, therapists, technicians, healthcare educators, social service professionals, non-clinical, home healthcare, dietitians, nutritionists, technicians, therapists, technologists, physicians, surgeons, researchers, nurses, and more.

Positions in Healthcare and related fields are ranked among the fastest growing in the United States, according to the Department of Labor. There will be an increase of positions due to demand to replace current openings after worker retirement and new openings will continue to emerge. The working conditions for positions in healthcare related fields are varied in facilities that operate 24-hours. Commonly, hospital rooms and critical care units are where the jobs can be found. However, do not underestimate the opportunities that may lie outside of the hospital, such as retirement communities, schools, and private homes.

For additional information about nursing and related healthcare careers, see below:

American Association of Nurses
www.nursingworld.org

American Association of Colleges of Nursing
www.aacn.nche.edu

Emergency Nurses Association
www.ena.org

American Radiological Nurses Association
www.arna.net

National Council of State Boards of Nursing
www.ncsbn.org

More Helpful Websites
National League of Nursing
www.nln.org

National League of Nursing Accrediting Commission, Inc.
www.nlnac.org

Commission on Graduates of Foreign Nursing Schools
www.cgfns.org

Nursing Career Center
www.medi-smart.com

Jobs in Healthcare
www.healthcareerweb.com

Healthcare Resources
www.healthcareresources.com

Healthcare Magazine
www.modernhealthcare.com

Nurse Week: Nursing Jobs
www.2nurseweek.com

Pharmacy Week
www.pweek.com

Work for Physicians
www.practiceline.com

More Helpful Websites
Careers in Biotechnology
www.biocareer.com
www.biohealthrx.com

Top Healthcare Careers
www.healthcareersusa.com
www.drofficejobs.com

Aging
National Hospice and Palliative Care Organization
www.nhpco.org

Geriatric Nursing Resources
www.geronurseonline.org

Gerontological Society of America
www.agework.com

Job #3

Mental Health Counselor

Counselors and therapists can work in multiple settings and based on the numbers; this work will be abundant. According to the National Alliance on Mental Illness, millions are impacted by mental illness; 1 out of 5 U.S. adults (57.8 million in 2021) experience mental illness each year and 1 out of 6 youth between ages 6-17 have been diagnosed with a disorder. If you are interested in joining the fight to help these populations and more with better resources or access, learn where to find the jobs and get them.

Job Overview

The mental health professional can include titles, like therapist, counselor, or practitioner. These professionals can work with people with substance abuse, family, and behavioral issues at schools, private practices, companies, and virtually.

Education Requirements (minimum): Multiple degrees may be required; master's and doctoral degrees with certifications.

Salary Range: $44,090- 86,480
(www.dol.gov)

For additional information about careers in mental health, see some helpful websites listed below:

www.betterhelp.com
Online therapy directory and resources along with job opportunities can be found on the website.

www.mentalhealthwork.com
The job site for mental health careers.

www.ihirementalhealth.com
Find job opportunities and career advice.
www.apa.org
The American Psychological Association offers a directory of reputable counselors and therapists, videos, training, magazines, journals, and newsletters.

www.treatment.gov
This portal could be your answer to find mental health resources and jobs.

www.findsupport.gov
Another one linked to the USA is findsuppot.gov. This is an online guide and community.

www.psychiatrictimes.com
The Psychiatric Times is a monthly publication for psychiatrist; a great resource.

Job #4

Chef/Food Manager

Increasingly, interest has been sparked in the food and related industries. More frequently than ever before individuals are dining out, ordering in, or placing requests with personal chefs and restaurants. There has also been a peak in food safety and nutritional factors, like American obesity related to food intake, as pronounced by media-induced attention.

We have also seen the growth of the cable channel, the Food Network® with famed chefs and entrepreneurs, Emeril, and cannot forget about chef and talk show host, Rachael Ray, all known for their tasty treats and big personalities. The vlogging and reality TV bug has hit the food industry glamorizing the industry, and soaring by allowing ice cream lovers and food designers to create the next new ice cream flavor with the *Haagen Daz's® Special* ; while *Hell's Kitchen,* offers an opportunity for aspiring chefs to battle for the "Top Chef" title.

As the center of every social gathering, many heads of households, administrative professionals, caterers, and coordinators enjoy the challenge to top last month's event by planning what's next on the menu. It's no shock that exploration in the industry's careers extend beyond food handling and preparation. They range from chef, nutritionist, food scientists, engineers, restaurant management, advisors, food writers, food truck owners, and more. Below, this section will focus on sources for a career as a chef and other food related jobs. Many careers in food have greater earning potential ranging to nearly six figure salaries.

Educational Requirements (minimum): Up to 2 year or 4 year programs at vocational schools and colleges

Salary Range: $38-$104K/yr, varies based on setting, chain, ownership (www.dol.gov)

Job Overview:

The best paid chefs and managers offer food preparation creating an atmosphere turning food into lifestyle art displays, while attempting to add nutritional value; although, sometimes defying nutritional guidelines for the sake of beauty.
Many contact them for help with daily meals and special events for all occasions, like assisting with catering needs for weddings, holiday parties, and reunions. They also prepare wanted menu items at upscale restaurants, hotels, resorts, and destination cruise ships. They may also venture into business ownership or franchising, for instance, independent catering companies, gift basket preparers, personal chef, concierge servicing, and owners of restaurants, bistros, or cafés. Other career and business opportunities also exist for those who cannot cook but enjoy the atmosphere that can only be found with entertainment.

For additional information about careers in food, see helpful websites listed below:

American Personal Chef Association
www.personalchef.com

American Culinary Federation
www.acfrchefs.org

More Helpful Websites

World Association of Chef's Societies and Schools
www.wac2000.org

National Restaurant Association
www.restaurant.org

National Restaurant Association and Educational Foundation
www.nraef.org

American Society of Agronomy
www.agronomy.org

American Society of Farm Managers and Rural Appraisers
www.asfmra.org

Food Network Magazine
www.foodnetwork.com

International Council on Hotel, Restaurants, and Institutions
Education
www.chrie.org

American Institute of Baking
www.aibonline.org

Food Marketing Institute
www.fmi.org

Franchise Information
www.franchoice.com

www.franchise.org

www.franchiseexpo.com

www.careersinfood.com

www.bigcitychefs.com

www.starchefs.com

www.foodindustryjobs.com

www.foodservice.com

www.hospitalityhr.com

www.caterer.com

Beverages
www.beverageworld.com

www.beverageonline.com

www.winejobs.com

www.probrewer.com

Baking
www.pastryscoop.com

www.bakery-net.com

Job #5

Technical Engineer

Although up until this point, referring to the basics has been discussed. Consider the future trends and needs of technology and artificial intelligence within our lives as you look for your next job. We cannot seem to do much without understanding how to use computers and apps from grocery shopping to renting a car or requesting a rideshare service. Sought after tech jobs include web developer, information security analyst, and data scientist.

Job Overview
Machine learning engineering or technical engineering are in demand. There are many job titles, but we'll discuss 3.

Web Developer- Creates and maintains websites, including visibility and user-friendliness.

Information Security Analyst- Protects companies' most sensitive information, networks, and systems.

Data Scientist- The ability to analyze data, like statistics and technical information and its implication to business to support better decision-making and operations.

Education Requirements:
Bachelor's degree for most, a certification fan be expected. Master's degree is often required for the data analyst role.

Salary Range (median): Web Developer ($77, 830), Information Security Analyst ($102,600), Data Scientist ($100,910)
(www.dol.gov)

For additional information about resources or options for career opportunities in tech, see below:

www.codepath.org
The website has early career tech talent matching and sometimes a summit.

www.dice.com
One of the oldest tech careers and news platforms. See the job board to find different jobs.

www.crunchboard.com
The official job board for TechCrunch. Shares job openings in IT, tech, and software development.

Volunteering

Volunteering may allow an opportunity for the big break you need for your next job opportunity while supporting a hobby or interest. One of the best resources for volunteerism can be found at www.energizeinc.com.

1-800-VOLUNTEER.org
http://www.1-800-volunteer.org
Portal site connects agencies that have online databases for volunteer opportunities. Offers a single source for posting and viewing opportunities by city.

CharityAmerica.com
http://www.charityamerica.com
Nonprofits register for online donations and post their volunteer opportunities.

Volunteer America
http://volunteer.gov/gov/
Web portal for federal government volunteer opportunities in the U.S. Departments of Agriculture, Defense, Interior, and Veterans Affairs, and the Corporation for National and Community Service, U.S. Army Corps of Engineers, and U.S.A. Freedom Corps. Opportunities to volunteer through a variety of government agencies. Check out the partners' list at
http://www.volunteer.gov/gov/partners.cfm

Community Leadership
The Community Leadership Association (formerly NACLO - National Association of Community Leadership Organizations)
http://www.communityleadership.org/

Planet Volunteer
http://www.planetfriendly.net/volunteer/
A web site linking individuals looking to volunteer with non-profits in their area looking for help.

Volunteer Solutions
http://www.volunteersolutions.org
Portal helps local non-profit agencies connect individuals to volunteer opportunities in their communities.

Make A Difference Day
http://www.usaweekend.com/diffday/
Sponsored by USA Weekend. Includes a database of volunteer opportunities for the Day.

Accountants

Accountants for the Public Interest (API)
http://www.geocities.com/api_woods/api/apihome.html

Arts

Opera Volunteers International
www.operavol.org

Volunteering for Students

Campus Compact
http://www.compact.org
Features hundreds of national colleges and universities committed to developing student civic values, service-learning, and school-community partnerships. Listing of state affiliates at http://www.compact.org/state/.

Idealist on Campus
http://www.idealistoncampus.org/
(Formerly COOL Campus Outreach Opportunity League)
Offers resources, events, educational tools, networking opportunities, and other programs that support students and campuses in strengthening communities through service, activism, and civic engagement.

School Break Missions
http://www.alternativebreaks.org
A site promoting quality university semester break experiences.

Young Volunteers
http://www.youngvolunteers.com/
Encourages young people to volunteer and promote ongoing, informed, interactive volunteerism.

Internships

Handshake
https://joinhandshake.com
Welcomes posting of internships of all kinds for students and graduates.

Chegg Internships
https://www.internships.com
Employers post various job openings.

InternshipPrograms.com
http://internships.wetfeet.com/Employers.asp
Commercial site specifically focused on internships, both paid and unpaid.

Education
National Association of Partners in Education, Inc. (NAPE)
http://www.NAPEhq.org

National Society for Experiential Education (NSEE)
http://www.nsee.org/

Volunteer Opportunities in Government and Law

Federal Interagency Team on Volunteerism (FITV)
http://www.volunteer.gov/fitv/index.html
For federally administered volunteer programs focused on preserving natural and cultural resources.

Federal Volunteer Administrators Network (FedVAN)
http://www.pointsoflight.org/networks/nonprofitgov/federal.cfm

National Association of Volunteer Programs in Local Government (NAVPLG)
http://www.navplg.org/
See website for the most current contact information.

Justice
Volunteers in Police Service (VIPS)
http://www.policevolunteers.org/
National site of the United States Dept. of Justice connecting local volunteer programs with police departments.

Volunteers in Prevention, Probation and Prisons, Inc.
http://vipmentoring.org/

Lawyers

American Bar Association Standing Committee on Pro Bono Public Services
http://www.abanet.org/legalservices/probono/volunteer.html
Includes links to other pro bono legal sites around the country:
http://www.abanet.org/legalservices/probono/directory/programlinks.html

Additional Volunteering Resources

Volunteer Lawyers for the Arts
http://www.starvingartistslaw.com/help/volunteer%20lawyers.htm
List of organizations in US cities maintained by the National
Endowment for the Arts

Libraries
Friends of Libraries USA
http://www.folusa.com/

Museums
American Association for Museum Volunteers (AAMV)
http://www.aamv.org/

World Leisure and Recreation Association (WLRA)'s Volunteer
Commission
http://www.worldleisure.org/about/interest_groups/volunteerism.htm
l
The WLRA has instituted the Volunteerism Commission, for a two-
year provisional period, to advance theoretical and practical
knowledge of the leisure aspects of volunteerism.

Online Volunteering Service

http://www.onlinevolunteering.org
A free service provided by the United Nations Volunteers program
that connects development organizations with online volunteers.
Volunteers can apply to hundreds of online opportunities.
Organizations can post assignments and access worldwide expertise.

Health & Fitness Volunteering Options

American Society for Directors of Volunteer Services (ASDVS) - USA
http://www.asdvs.org

For practitioners in hospitals and nursing homes. An affiliate group of the American Hospital Association.

YMCA
The YMCA offers multiple developmental and recreational programs for youth and adults. If interested in becoming a lifeguard or learning about CPR, this agency can help you too.

HealthCare Volunteer
http://www.healthcarevolunteer.com
A free portal to connect health professionals to volunteer opportunities around the world. Organizations may post opportunities to recruit health care volunteers. See the instructions at http://healthcarevolunteer.com/organizations/.

MD Charity Match
http://www.mdcharitymatch.com
Assists medical doctors with volunteer positions anywhere in the world.

Opportunities Working with and for Seniors

AmeriCorps Seniors
https://americorps.gov
Senior volunteers, 55+ are matched with service.

AARP
https://www.aarp.org
Nonprofit offers multiple senior resources, including job search options for seniors or jobs working with them.

GuideStar
http://www.guidestar.org/classifieds
A complete guide of charities to target and inform donors of various programs and charity performance in the U.S.

Mentoring

International Mentoring Association
http://www.mentoring-association.org/

My Brother's Keeper Alliance
www.obama.org

Big Brothers Big Sisters
www.bbbs.org

National Mentoring Partnership
http://www.mentoring.org/
Site of a national network of mentoring organizations.

SCORE
Agency offers free start-up business mentoring or low-cost business advice and training from experts https://www.score.org

Board Participation Opportunities

Boardnet USA
http://www.boardnetusa.org
Connects potential board members to nonprofit, charitable organizations. Organizations can post their board member vacancies for view.

BoardSource (formerly National Center for Nonprofit Boards)
http://www.boardsource.org

-BONUS SECTION-

Business Social Etiquette:

Solutions for Good Habits, Appetizers, and Finger Foods for Potlucks and Business Social Events

Meetings surrounding food are all too common at work. I have prepared a list of six simple steps to keep you on the "A" list at every business social.

First rule do not appear empty handed or with dirty hands. Everyone appreciates cleanliness. No one wants to eat from the co-worker with filthy hands, unclean fingernails, or the one who displays untidiness.

Secondly, bring a dish. Prepare food that is easy to transport and can be quickly prepared. If you burn your planned dish or cannot cook, please arrive with your store bought dish. Just as no one wants to smell burnt food, no one wants to eat it either.

Thirdly, respect others by not over eating and avoid double dipping and finger-licking.

Fourth rule; use the time to engage in work-friendly conversation. Get to know your "neighbors." Meet new employees and employees in other departments. Avoid cliques.

Fifth rule; offer your assistance during clean-up time. At minimum, remove your dish and make sure your eating area is clean prior to your departure.

Lastly, thank the organizer for the invitation.   Once you follow these easy steps, you will be worthy of a second invite.

To take the worries out of your planning and your dish preparation, I have included some of my favorite recipes that are perfect for potluck dinner parties or anytime you want a good snack.

8 Recipes for Potluck Social Gatherings

Seafood Pizza Bread

Summary of Ingredients:
1 can of diced tomatoes
½ can of tomato paste
1 cup of mozzarella cheese
1 teaspoon of cilantro
1 teaspoon of oregano
1 teaspoon parsley
1 teaspoon of basil
2 loaves of garlic bread
½ cup of crawfish tails (optional)
1 8 oz bag of John Soules® Fajita Chicken breast (strips or chunks optional)
1 small package of pepperoni (optional)
½ lb. of shrimp, cooked and deveined
1/3 cup of water

Preparation Time: 15 minutes
Cook Time: Oven (10 minutes) or Microwave (1-2 minutes)

Mix tomato paste, 1/3 cup of water, parsley, basil, cilantro in a large bowl. Layer garlic bread with tomato paste. Rinse crawfish tails. Place crawfish tails in pot of water covering all tails with water, (approximately 2 cups of water) and heat for 5-7 minutes. Place clean, rinsed cooked shrimp, without tail in a different small pot of water; making sure water covers all shrimp. Heat for 5 minutes. Drain water in shrimp and crawfish. Heat chicken breast strips for 2 minutes in another bowl. On garlic layered side of bread, sprinkle shrimp, diced tomatoes, crawfish, chicken breast strips (dicing is optional). Top with cheese. Slice in portions. One loaf may prepare appetizers for 6-8. Place in oven 350 degrees for 5-10 minutes or microwave for 1-2 minutes or until cheese is melted. If you plan to take to work, the microwave will work best. Heat at work, verses heating at home. Use the microwave just before the beginning of your social. Place prepared pizza bread on microwavable plates to heat and melt cheese, 1 minute Bring your decorative tray after heating and prepare to serve. Do not overheat to allow freshness.

Speechless Spicy Wings

Summary of Ingredients:
1 family pack of chicken wings
½ cup of Worcheshire sauce
1/3 cup of Teriyaki sauce (optional)
2 tbsp cooking oil, butter, or olive oil
2 tbsp mix of your favorite blended mix (Accent®, Lawry's®, etc.)
4 teaspoon garlic salt
2 teaspoon basil
4 teaspoon cayenne pepper, optional

Preparation Time: 10 Minutes
Cook Time: 1 Hour 15 Minutes, approx.

Heat oven at 350 degrees F. Rinse chicken wings with water. Place 1tbsp or cooking oil, butter, or olive oil at bottom of large pan, layered with foil. Place chicken in pan with water and oil. Add ½ of all dry seasoning ingredients (basil, cayenne pepper, garlic salt, and seasoning mix) to back side on chicken. Bake for 20 minutes. Remove from the oven. Turn chicken overusing thongs to front side. Layer chicken add (Teriyaki sauce optional), Worcheshire® sauce, and then add 2 teaspoons of dry seasoning (garlic salt and cayenne pepper) or season to taste. Bake for another 30-40 minutes. Continue checking for to prevent burning. Chicken will appear blackened, however, remove before burnt scent. Let cool for atleast 15 minutes and serve.

Crab Bites

Summary of Ingredients:
2 packages of croissants or crackers
½ can of Rotel® diced tomatoes
1-2 cans of crab meat
1 can or package of spinach or artichoke dip
¼ cup of green onions
1 cup of cream cheese
1 teaspoon of salt, optional
1 teaspoon of pepper
½ teaspoon of garlic salt & garlic powder

Preparation Time: 10 Minutes
Cook Time: 20 Minutes, approx.

Place spinach or artichoke dip in sauce pan for approximately 5-8 minutes. Pour cut corn in a second sauce pan on low heat for 5-8 minutes or until warm. Dice green onions.   In a large bowl, blend cream cheese, garlic salt, garlic powder, crab meat, green onions, spinach or artichoke dip, and mix for 1 minute, until smoothly blended. The mixture will be layered on crackers or croissants. Sprinkle Rotel® tomatoes, garlic salt, Take croissants and cut the corners or use crackers, no cutting. After you have mixed all ingredients, spread on croissants. Slice in small portions, halves or thirds.   Should appear like mini bite-sized flaky sandwiches or cracker sandwiches. Add colorful toothpicks in each piece of croissant, optional. Place on decorative tray.

Meat Lover's Macho Nachos

Summary of Ingredients:
1 can of Rotel® tomatoes (Mexican style)
1 large package of Velveeta® cheese
1 can of Campbell's® cheddar cheese
1 ½ cups of water
1/3 cup of white onion, chopped
1/3 cup of chopped green onion
1 lb of ground beef or ground turkey, rinsed
1 package of Taco Seasoning mix
1 lb bag of tortilla chips
1 8 oz bag of John Soules® Fajita Chicken breast (strips or chunks)
1 package of shredded Cheddar or Colby cheese (optional)

Preparation Time: 10 minutes
Cook Time: 35 minutes

In a large saucepan, add beef or turkey with white onions, green onions, and taco seasoning mix and brown well done, not burnt. Add cheese, water, and in large pot and heat until melted. Add more water, if needed. Blend chicken and turkey or beef in cheese mixture all together in the large pot. Continue to heat turn down to low. Pour cheese in large serving bowl or container or take along in crock pot with tortilla chips in serving tray or paper towel layered wicker basket for display. Or layer tray with tortilla chips, top with melted cheese and meat mixture then sprinkle some of the Rotel® and shredded cheese. Use a large spoon for serving.

Pasta Salad

Summary of Ingredients:
1 12 oz. bag of twirl or garden colorful noodles
½-1 cup of Italian salad dressing
¼ cup of black olives, garnish
¼ cup of shredded parmesan cheese
1 bag of pepperoni
1 can of chicken chunks
1 can on ham chunks
½ of diced tomatoes
1 tbsp of basil
1 teaspoon of salt
1 teaspoon of celery salt, garnish (optional)
1 teaspoon of chives, garnish (optional)
1 head of lettuce (optional)
8 Bell peppers (use same # as people serving)

Preparation Time: 10 Minutes
Cook Time: 10 Minutes

Boil water adding pasta or noodles and salt. Boil until soft or approximately 10 minutes. Strain to eliminate water and run cold water on noodles. Allow to cool. Pour in large bowl mixing and adding all meat (pepperoni, chicken chunks, ham chunks). Sprinkle celery salt, basil, and salad dressing to taste. Toss salad. Garnish with olives, parmesan cheese, and chives.   Serve in large serving bowl or serve individually on tray on top of lettuce leaves or inside of carved and hollowed bell pepper.

Meatball Melt

Summary of Ingredients:
Meatballs
1 lb of ground beef
1 cup of cheddar cheese chunks (jalapeno cheese or mozzarella)
1 tbsp of each (blended seasoning, like McCormick's®, salt, pepper, and basil
1tbsp garlic, chopped or garlic powder

Sauce
1 cup of barbecue sauce
4 teaspoons honey mustard
1/3 cup of apple cider vinegar
1 teaspoon lemon or orange juice
1 teaspoon hot sauce (Louisiana Hot Sauce®)

Preparation Time: 15 minutes
Cook Time: 7-10 minutes

Cheese-filled Meatballs
Rinse and season beef with salt, pepper, chopped garlic or garlic powder, and basil. Using a rolling pin or glass, roll beef on flat surface, like patties. Place cheese chunk in center. Create small balls walnut size by rolling in palm of hand. Place in large heated frying pan without oil. Brown on all sides until done. Allow to cool, 5-minutes.

Sauce
Pour sauce ingredients in small serving bowl and blend. Use as dip.
Place meatballs on tray surrounding dip. Or add meatballs to the
sauces.

Coco-Choco Chews

Summary of Ingredients:
1 16 oz. bag of large marshmallows
3 large Hershey® bars
1 bag of Nestle® chocolate chips
1 bag of Trail mix
½ cup of shredded coconut, optional

Preparation Time: 10 minutes
Cook Time: 3 minutes

Melt all chocolate in large sauce pan for approximately 5-7 minutes
or until melted. Place marshmallows in large bowl, adding trail mix
and coconut. Pour melted chocolate on top and mix quickly. Place
cooking sheet or wax paper on a flat surface and spoon. Shape into
small to mid-sized balls or circles of chocolate on sheet. Let cool.
Place in refrigerator for 10 minutes or until ready to serve. Layer or
place in candy dish or decorative container.

Gourmet Dipped Pretzels

Summary of Ingredients:
1 box of your favorite pretzels
1 lb or bar of semi-sweet chocolate, for baking and candy purposes
1 cup of decorative candies (ex: colorful sprinkles)
1 cup of chopped nuts or nut pieces

Preparation Time: 5 minutes
Cook Time: 5-10 minutes

Melt all chocolate in medium sized saucepan for approximately 5-10 minutes or until melted on low heat. Do not overheat. Place wax paper or foil paper on flat surface. Spread toppings (candies and nuts) on different sheets of wax paper or foil. Dip pretzels in chocolate using a fork or tongs. Remove excess and lay on toppings. Sprinkle toppings on top. Toppings should appear on all sides of pretzels. Refrigerate for 5 minutes. Remove from refrigerator and gently remove all excess to shape perfectly. Place in container or on decorative tray.

Disclaimer

The content of this guide is to prepare the job seeker or dissatisfied employee with a basic understanding of job searching tips and tips for survival in the interim. The author, Career Wit Consulting (DBA, Career Wit), affiliates, companies, websites, sources listed are not responsible for the outcome and consequences of the application of the content provided. Results will vary. Discretion and caution should be used prior to purchasing service from service providers when submitting personal information in any method; electronically, face-to-face, by phone to any of the fore mentioned websites and companies.

Other Career Wit Products and Services
(**www.careerwit.com**):

Career Wit Kit™: A Comprehensive Career Management Camp

☐ E-Workshop-Job Search Safety (Online self-paced training)
☐ Personal Consultations (Optional Career Wit Consultant
   assistance, applicable additional fee)
☐ E-book, *Guide to Managing Your Job Search*
☐ E-book, *Career Wit Time Management Journal*
☐ Career Wit Exclusive Self-service Center Access

OnDemand Training Programs
When getting started with your job search and within your career,
we recommend that you especially utilize the online training that is
offered, self-study or consultant-led. There are many to choose from.
Ongoing continuing education and training supports prospective
employers, and later advancing in your career.

Consulting
Independent consultants are also available to partner with you as
questions may arise during your search. Some of the services our
consultants offer include resume writing and critique, interview
preparation with mock or practice interview sessions, personal
shopping guidance and business etiquette.

Greeting Cards
Career Wit offers work related greeting cards designed to celebrate a
job promotion or retirement; request an interview, or reward a job
well done.

www.careerwit.com

www.ingramcontent.com/pod-product-compliance
Lightning Source LLC
Chambersburg PA
CBHW060347130626
46553CB00003B/1122